D1509023

To:

From:

Date:

The Two of Us

A Book About Dogs and Their Owners

Ellen Small
James Dale

STARK BOOKS

Andrews McMeel
Publishing

Kansas City

The Two of Us: A Book About Dogs and Their Owners

For information, write Andrews McMeel Publishing,
an Andrews McMeel Universal company, 4520 Main Street,
Kansas City, Missouri 64111.

ISBN 0-7407-1043-5

Library of Congress Catalog Card Number: 00-108492

Book design by Holly Camerlinck

Book composition by Kelly & Company, Lee's Summit, Missouri

—— *Attention: Schools and Businesses* ——

Andrews McMeel books are available at quantity discounts with bulk purchase for educational,
business, or sales promotional use. For information, please write to: Special Sales Department,
Andrews McMeel Publishing, 4520 Main Street, Kansas City, Missouri 64111.

The Two of Us

The two of us . . .

. . . sometimes wake up with morning breath.

The two of us . . .

. . . like to stay in bed on
Sunday and read the paper.

The two
of us . . .

. . . do not like to
be left home alone.

The two of us . . .

. . . will jump into a pile of leaves just because it's there.

The two of us . . .

. . . bring each other stuff.

The two of us . .

. . . are always
happy to see
each other.

The two of us . . .

. . . like to run through sprinklers.

The two
of us . . .

. . . are always
hungry.

The two of us . . .

. . . can't resist leftovers.

The two of us . . .

. . . like to
dig up
cool stuff.

The two of us . . .

. . . love to go for long walks on the beach.

. . . are natural-born dog-paddlers.

The two of us . . .

. . . think puddles are
for stepping in, not over.

The two
of us . . .

. . . think Dog-and-
Owner Frisbee
should be an
Olympic sport.

The two of us . . .

. . . sometimes forget to wipe
our feet before we come inside.

The two of us . . .

. . . can
get really
dirty.

The two of us . . .

. . . like to stick our heads
out car windows.

The two of us . .

. . . are bold wilderness explorers.

The two of us . . .

. . . count everything in dog years.

The two of us . . .

. . . never get tired of playing "fetch."

The two of us . . .

. . . love midnight snacks (and morning,
noon, afternoon, early evening,
and before-bed snacks).

The two of us . . .

. . . hate the phrase "bad dog."

The two of us . . .

. . are fiercely loyal (but not very fierce).

The two of us . . .

. . . don't understand why <u>101 Dalmatians</u>
didn't win the Oscar for Best Picture.

The two of us . . .

. . . like to dry off using the "shaking" method.

The two
of us . . .

. . . look guilty
when we've been bad.

The two of us . . .

. . . run until we're out of breath
and then drink water really loudly.

. . . don't look good in hats.

The two of us . . .

. . . believe in old values like loyalty,
friendship, trust, and getting
a biscuit for being good.

The two of us . . .

. . . look out for each other.

The two of us . . .

. . . like the same TV shows
(anything where the dog is the hero).

The two of us . .

. . . have a bark worse than our bite.

The two of us . . .

. . . love commercials with dogs
(especially the ones where the dogs talk).

The two of us . . .

. . . can sleep all day (and still sleep all night).

The two of us . . .

. . . dance around when we
have to go to the bathroom.

. . . like to stake out our territory.

The two of us . . .

. . . hate leashes because we
always get tangled up in them.

The two of us . . .

. . . can't wait for the mailman to come.

The two
of us . . .

. . . don't always
come when
we're called.

The two of us . . .

. . . are scared of thunder
(and sometimes hide under the bed).

. . . like
people food
better than
dog food.

The two of us . . .

. . . will never be alone.

The two of us . . .

. . . love Halloween because you
wear costumes and get treats.

The two of us . . .

. . . like to be scratched on our bellies.

The two of us . . .

. . . just like to be scratched.

The two of us . . .

. . . are more mutt than purebred.

The two of us . . .

. . . like how we look after we get our hair done.

The two of us . . .

. . . think it would be really cool
to hang around fire stations.

The two of us . . .

. . . have been told we look alike.

The two of us . . . . don't like to get shots.

The two
of us . . .

. . . are antifence.

The two of us . . .

. . . cringe when we hear the word "Rennel."

The two of us . . .

NO DOGS
ALLOWED ON BEACH
MAY 15 - SEPT. 30
$50.00 FINE

. . . are pro-animal
rights (except cats).

The two of us . . .

. . . believe in Santa Claus.

The two
of us . . .

. . . believe in
puppy love.

The two of us . . .

. . . like big, wet kisses.

The two of us . . .

. . . will answer to any name if
the person calling us has a treat.

lead a dog's life

The two of us . . .